Friends in Need

by Paul Meeks
illustrated by Doug Jarmin

Harcourt

Orlando   Boston   Dallas   Chicago   San Diego

Visit *The Learning Site!*
www.harcourtschool.com

Only certain kinds of dogs are chosen to be trained to help people who cannot see. Such dogs must be intelligent, alert, and willing to learn. They must also be strong, healthy, and calm. Another important quality is that they must enjoy working with people. A guide dog must have a certain amount of bulk so that it will be strong enough to lead a person.

Golden retrievers, Labrador retrievers, and German shepherds all make good guide dogs because they often have these qualities. Other kinds of dogs sometimes become guides, but most guide dogs come from these three breeds.

The selection of a guide dog often begins before it is even born, when its mother is chosen. Females that have all the desired qualities are often retired from the training program so they can have puppies. It is hoped that the puppies will have the mother's good qualities.

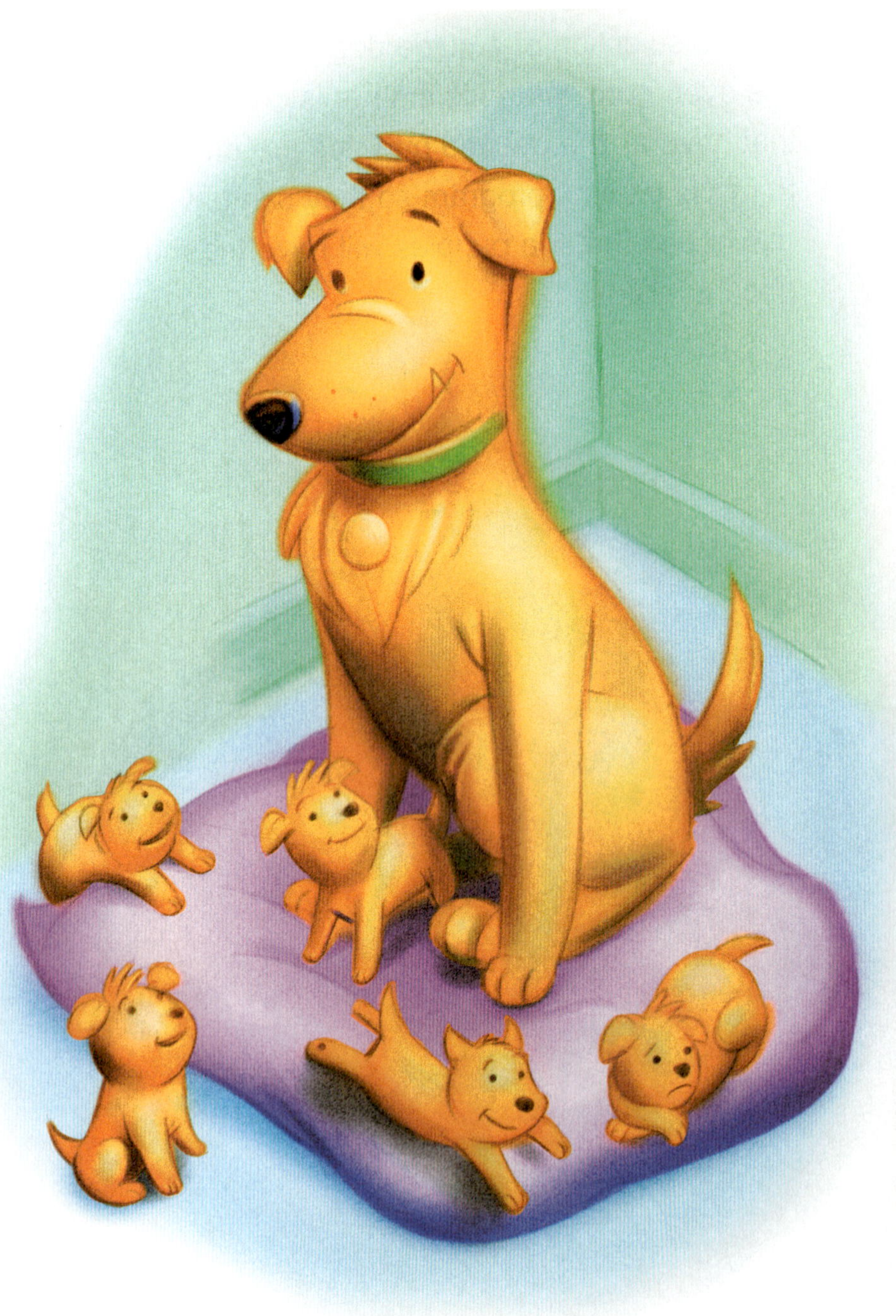

There are many different training centers for guide dogs. Some trainers believe that puppies should be born and raised in private homes before they begin their training. Other trainers care for the mothers in the training center before the puppies are born. They then take care of the mothers and puppies for the first six weeks of the puppies' lives.

After a puppy is born, it stays with its mother for about six weeks. When the puppy is six to eleven weeks old, it is tested and observed. Even though the mother might be an excellent dog, not every puppy of hers is chosen to be a guide dog. Some dogs might be too small, too cautious, or too easily frightened. These dogs might make good pets, but they would not be good guide dogs.

Before the puppy is twelve weeks old, it gets all the shots and other medical attention it needs. Its health is checked to make sure that no physical problems will keep it from doing its job.

By the time it is about twelve weeks old, the puppy is ready for the second stage of its training. After that, the training center may send the puppies to private homes so they can get used to people. Living in private homes helps the dogs grow up to be friendly and at ease with people. For the next year, the dog learns to get along with people. It lives with a family while it grows up. The family gives the dog as many different experiences as possible. In this way, the dog gets used to handling itself in many situations.

The dog is trained to behave and to obey simple commands, like *come, sit, lie down,* and *stay*. Most important of all, it learns how to act when it is out in the community. It's allowed to go places where other animals are pointedly forbidden to enter. It learns not to snort at distractions, such as other dogs. One very well-trained guide dog was once said to have resembled a statue after it was told to sit. It is this kind of training that prepares an excitable puppy to be a calm adult dog.

At about twelve to eighteen months, the dog is ready for its real education to start. If it has been living with a family, the family must disengage itself from the dog. Although the family members are sad and will miss the dog, they know that they have helped the dog on its way to being a good guide.

The family takes the dog to the training center. The dog is measured and weighed. Then a veterinarian examines the dog to make sure it is healthy. The vet even X-rays the dog's hips to make sure no problems keep it from walking properly.

Some dogs do not measure up to all the standards, either physically or in training. If this happens, the dog is put up for adoption. The family that took care of the dog as a puppy gets the first chance to ask to keep the dog as a pet.

Even though a dog might have to be retired from the program, it may still make an excellent pet. Standards for guide dogs are very high. In fact, only about 50 percent of the dogs that start the program finish it.

The next stage of a guide dog's training takes five to seven months. A trainer is assigned to each dog. That trainer teaches the dog everything it will need to know to guide a person who is blind.

At first, the trainer uses a leash when taking the dog out for walks. Later, the dog is trained to get used to the harness. This is similar to a leash, except that instead of going around the dog's neck, it goes around the dog's body. Attached to the harness is a long handle that the trainer holds.

The dog must learn to walk in a straight line on the left side of the trainer, stopping whenever it comes to a curb. If the trainer says "Hup, hup!" and swings an arm forward, the dog learns that this means to go forward. The dog also learns "intelligent disobedience." This means that if it is not safe to go forward, the dog will refuse to move.

A guide dog learns that there is a time to play and a time to work. While working, the dog must not pay any attention to squirrels, pigeons, cats, or other dogs. A guide dog must also learn to pointedly ignore people who might want to pet it while it is working. As long as the dog is in the harness, it is working. Someone must disengage the harness before the guide dog can play.

A guide dog must also look out for obstacles overhead. For example, even though the dog can easily walk under low branches, its owner—who cannot see the obstacles—might bump into them and get hurt. The guide dog learns to steer its owner past such obstacles.

The last stage of the training lasts about three or four weeks. People who want guide dogs come to the center where the dogs have been trained. There they are matched up to suitable dogs.

How does a trainer know how to match people and dogs? Well, a small, elderly person would not want a dog that is the size of a small horse. Such a person would do better with a less bulky dog—a smaller one that would be easier to handle.

For a few weeks, the people live at the training center and get to know their dogs. The dog's trainer helps during this period. All three—the dog, the trainer, and the new owner—go for walks around the grounds and in town. They go to malls, restaurants, and banks. They might even ride a train. The trainer watches closely to make sure that the dog and the new owner are communicating well.

Before the new owner takes the dog home, there is a graduation ceremony. The family that raised the dog as a puppy might even take part in the ceremony.

Finally, the day comes when the dog and the new owner go home. This might even involve a ride in an airplane, during which the dog sits on the floor at the owner's feet.

After about a week, the trainer makes a follow-up visit to the new owner's home to make sure everything is going well. From that point on, the dog and the new owner can look forward to many happy years together.